More Meditations
to Make You
SMILE

Martha J. Beckman
Illustrated by

DIMENSIONS
FOR LIVING

NASHVILLE

MORE MEDITATIONS TO MAKE YOU SMILE

Copyright © 1997 by Dimensions for Living

This book is printed on recycled, acid-free, elemental-clorine–free paper.

ISBN 0-687-00952-9

Scripture quotations, unless otherwise indicated, are from the New Revised Standard Version Bible, copyright © 1989, by the Division of Christian Education of the National Council of the Churches of Christ in the United States of America.

Scripture quotations noted NIV are taken from the Holy Bible: New International Version. Copyright © 1973, 1978, 1984 by the International Bible Society. Used by permission of Zondervan Bible Publishers.

97 98 99 00 01 02 03 04 05 06—10 9 8 7 6 5 4 3 2 1

MANUFACTURED IN THE UNITED STATES OF AMERICA

Editor's Note

This book is dedicated to the loving memory of Martha J. Beckman, who died prior to the publication of her first book, *Meditations to Make You Smile*. We are grateful to her three children, Nita Beckman, Phil Beckman, and Kathleen Blomquist, for their assistance in gathering material for this second volume. It is our hope that these humorous and inspirational insights will lift your spirit as they bring a smile to your face.

More Meditations
to Make You Smile

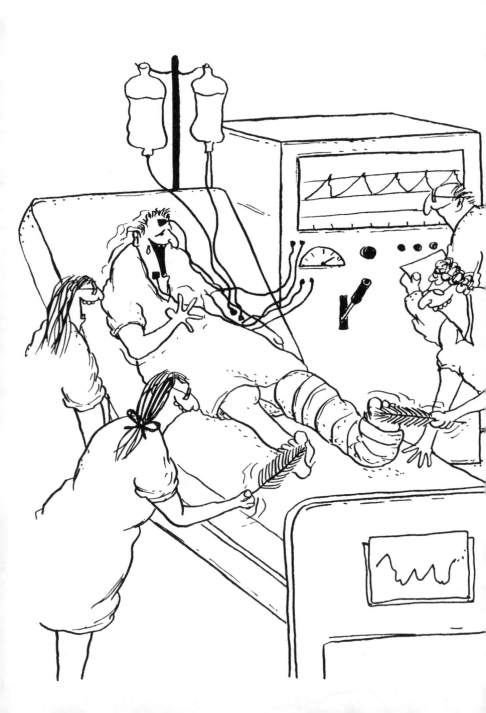

What is the longest word in the English language?

Smiles. There's a "mile" between the first and last letters!

One smile really can "go a long way." Scientists have proved that smiling and laughing are actually beneficial to our health. Why, then, in our health-conscious society do so many of us wear frowns on our faces so much of the time? Why don't we laugh more often?

Life's problems are no laughing matter, yet laughter puts sanity back into our living. Laughter eases our tension and helps us break rigid patterns of apathy and pessimism.

Go ahead, turn up those corners of your mouth! Smile! Laugh! Remember, "This is the day that the LORD has made; let us rejoice and be glad in it" (Psalm 118:24).

Thank you, God, for your gift of laughter. Help me to live joyfully each and every day.

A sign at a railroad crossing read, "The average time for the train to pass this crossing is 14 seconds, whether your car is on the track or not."

A woman stopped at a service station to ask for directions. Several people tried to tell her how to go, but she simply could not understand. Finally, a young man said, "Just follow me and I'll take you right there."

Signs and signals are posted on roads and railroad crossings to protect and guide us. Sometimes we ignore them, often to our own harm; at other times, we simply cannot understand what the signs mean. At those times, the only way out may be to follow a guide.

As we journey through life, we can be thankful that God provided a guide for us in the form of his Son. No matter how confusing the signs are along the way, we can be sure we will always be safely on the right road if we keep our eyes on Jesus.

Thank you, God, for sending your Son to show me the way.

A Little League coach was asked the name of his team. He replied, "The Scrambled Eggs."

"Oh? Why did you pick that name?" someone asked. He answered, "Because we're always getting beat!"

Some days it's almost impossible not to feel defeated. Go to any sporting event and you'll find plenty of people in the bleachers who know just how the players should be playing in order to win the game!

But those aren't the people who win. The team members on the field, playing in the hope of winning, are the real victors. The coach who can inspire players to that hope will often have a winning team.

When you have one of those down days, turn to God, read his Word for assurances of hope, and ask God to fill you with hope and peace.

Lord, fill my heart with your love. May I play the game of life joyfully, resting in your hope.

A man went to see the doctor for his annual physical exam. When he came home later that afternoon, his wife asked him, "What did the doctor say?"

He answered in a gruff voice, "He told me that if I want to stay healthy, I have to eat what I don't want, drink what I don't like, and do what I'd rather not!"

We are surrounded by things that are good for us and things that aren't. Leaders in science and religion give us clear guidelines to follow when making choices, but all too often we choose to ignore their suggestions. We eat the wrong foods or do not eat the right foods; we get too much or too little sleep and exercise; we spend too little time in prayer and contemplation and too much time being anxious.

Paul said, "The fruit of the Spirit is love, joy, peace, patience, kindness, generosity, faithfulness, gentleness, and self-control" (Galatians 5:22-23). When faced with making a decision, ask yourself which choice will bear good "fruit of the spirit."

Lord, you always know my needs. Help me always to choose what is truly good for me.

A little boy said to his friend, "My family is really out of it. We have a *cord* on our phone and a pencil sharpener you have to turn *by hand!*"

Our technological world seems to be moving faster than we can keep up! Just when we think we've acquired the latest gadgets, we discover that technology has raced on ahead and left us behind, standing in the dust.

With dizzying advances and changes happening all around us, it's reassuring to know that God never changes. God's love for us is as constant and predictable as the sun and the moon and the stars. No matter how different our world may be in five, ten, or twenty years, we can be sure that God will be with us, keeping us safe and secure in his loving care.

Thank you, God, for your constant presence and unchanging love.

Susan took one look at her friend's exhausted expression and cluttered office and said, "What you need is a vacation!"

Her overworked friend asked jokingly, "Vacation? What's that?"

"A vacation," Susan explained, "is what you take if you can no longer take what you've been taking!"

Deadlines rule our lives. We rush ahead, looking at calendars and schedules, hardly daring to breathe lest we miss our deadline. Finally, when we can no longer take what we've been taking, we stop for rest.

In Africa, when people go on a long hike they stop often to rest. "We must stop," they say, "and let our souls catch up." Resolve to give yourself a few minutes a day to let your soul catch up. Rest in God's Word; look out a window. There is sure to be evidence of God's wonderful creation no matter where you are. Take a short walk; smile at a friend, a colleague, or a stranger. You'll be surprised at how much you can get done!

Lord, slow me down. Let me rest in you so that my deadlines may become lifelines.

A little boy was listening in on a conversation between his mother and grandmother. The young mother said to the boy's grandmother, "You're not old, Mom, you're only sixty-five."

Her son, quite impressed, cried, "Grandma, you've reached the speed limit!"

What a difference it makes to see things through the eyes of a child! The daughter tried to give her mother reassurance, but the little boy responded with joy. Growing older may not seem to be a reason for rejoicing, but Paul reminds us that we are to "rejoice always, pray without ceasing, give thanks in all circumstances; for this is the will of God in Christ Jesus for you" (1 Thessalonians 5:16-18).

No matter what the circumstance, try to see with the eyes of a child. Look inside; feel the spirit of Christ within you. That's where you will find joy!

Thank you, Lord, for being the one who makes all things new. Help me find joy in all things.

McPherson

A young jogger took a seat next to an old man on a park bench. The old man looked up and said, "I'm in great shape, too. Every artery is hard as a rock!"

Exercise is essential for a healthy, fit body. The same is true of spiritual health and fitness. Just as sitting on a park bench day after day leads to atrophy and physical illness, so also sitting passively on a pew leads to malaise and spiritual disease. Good spiritual exercise includes Bible study, meditation, prayer, and service to others. The result is the joy of living the abundant life which God intends.

Give me the discipline I need to stay spiritually fit, Lord.

The doctor tried to place a stethoscope on the little girl's chest, telling her that he was going to listen to her heart.

"Oh, no!" the little girl protested. "My heart is in my back."

"Where did you get that idea?" the doctor asked.

"Well, when I do something good, Grandma pats me on the back and says, 'Bless your little heart.'"

Grandmas always seem to give their hearts to their grandchildren, don't they? Giving your heart to another is the most precious gift you can give.

Who is the person you have cared about the most in your lifetime? Who is the person you find the most difficult to love? Can you find in the second person some of the attributes you find in the first? Perhaps you can find within yourself attributes of the one you have cared about the most. If so, you may be on the road to extending your already established affection toward the one who is most difficult to love. The joy of being loved in return is reserved for those who offer their own unconditional love.

God of love, make me aware of the power of love in my life.

Seventy-five-year-old Bob bought a hairpiece, had a facelift, and worked out for six months in a gym. Then he invited a woman half his age to have dinner with him. As they were getting out of his new sports car, Bob was struck by lightning and died. When he got to heaven, he rushed up to the gate and said woefully, "Why me?"

Saint Peter replied, "Oh, Bob, we didn't recognize you!"

Often we wish we could be someone other than who we are. We don't like our hairline or the shape of our nose or our weight. So we get a hairpiece or a nose job. We wear clothing appropriate for youth, but not for aging gracefully. We pretend to be someone we're not. We might fool others—and even ourselves—but we can never fool God.

There is nothing wrong with self-improvement, but trying to become something other than the persons God created us to be is a senseless waste of energy. Remember, God loves *you*—just the way you are!

> *Dear God, help me be the person you created me to be.*

A sign in a dry cleaners read, "No matter how bad the stain is, we'll take it out . . . and sew up the hole."

We all have clothing stains that are impossible to remove. No matter how much stain remover we apply or how many times we soak and wash the items, they simply won't come clean. How disappointed we are when the stained item happens to be one of our favorite things to wear! With regret, we toss it aside, never to wear it again.

In a way, we're not unlike our clothes. There are stains in our lives that we can't seem to wash away. We try to remove them ourselves, and we end up making things worse—cutting holes in our lives and our relationships. But unlike the way we give up on our discarded stained and torn clothes, God never gives up on us. By his grace, he washes away our stains, our sins, and makes us clean. And like a skillfull seamstress, God sews up the holes we've made in our lives so that the "repairs" are invisible.

No matter how bad our "stains" may be, God can help. God will forgive us and make us whole. All we have to do is ask.

O God, please forgive me and make me whole.

27

A man walked up to the counter of an auto parts store and said, "I'd like to get a new gas cap for my old car."

"Sure," said the clerk. "Sounds like a fair exchange."

"What's it worth?" is a question we ask daily, whether we're buying something or deciding to spend time at some activity. An object's value or worth is truly in the eyes of the beholder.

What is the worth of the cross? Its use as an instrument of torture would have very little value for most of us. But when seen as the symbol of all that God in Christ has done for the world, its worth is invaluable. The cross "bought" us a lot: life, love, hope, salvation, and peace. These things were given to us freely, as precious gifts. When we receive them, our hearts overflow and we reach out to others, offering them that priceless treasure.

Lord, help me never to forget the price that Jesus paid for me. May I freely offer to others your priceless gifts.

Two men were talking about their problems while exercising at the gym. One said to the other, "Just when we learn to take things with a grain of salt, the doctor puts us on a salt-free diet!"

We often speak of a person's going from bad to worse, but we never seem to speak of a person's going from bad to good. Yet that is what is at the heart of the gospel. We can go from bad to good. Human nature can change for the better. Jesus knew this; he always looked beyond the distressing exterior of a person to what that person might become.

We can find solutions to our problems when we turn our rebellious nature over to God. There is always a way out. It may not be a smooth road, but God can help us find a solution if we will only let him.

Dear Lord, thank you for your loving forgiveness and for helping me become all that you created me to be.

All you men who like music, step forward two paces," the sergeant said.

Six men responded.

"Okay," the sergeant continued, "You six get busy and carry that piano up to the top floor of the officers' quarters!"

No doubt those six men were surprised at their sergeant's command! Yet as disciplined soldiers, they wouldn't even think of making excuses or arguing with their sergeant. They would simply do the work their sergeant had commanded them to do.

Should it be any different for us as Christians? If we profess to be followers of Christ, we are to do the work he has called us to do—enthusiastically and without question. What is that work? Jesus instructed his disciples, "Go therefore and make disciples of all nations . . . teaching them to obey everything that I have commanded you" (Matthew 28:19-20). In other words, we are to share the love of Christ with everyone we meet. We are to be imitators of Christ, patterning our lives after his example and helping others come to know him.

O Lord, help me to be your faithful disciple today and every day.

Two men had just met at a party. "What do you do for a living?" one asked the other.

"I work in a clock factory," he replied.

"Oh? And what exactly do you do?" the first man asked.

"Just stand around all day and make faces," he said with a smile.

Doesn't it seem that some people just "stand around all day and make faces"? We wonder why they aren't as conscientious or productive or efficient or disciplined or serious as we are. We dismiss them as being lazy or silly—or perhaps even inferior. We pat ourselves on the back, congratulating ourselves for being concerned about the important things in life. But are we?

Often we become so consumed with the busyness of our days that we leave little or no time for simply enjoying God's gift of life. God wants us to live joyfully every day—whatever our circumstances may be. How are you doing?

God, fill me to overflowing with your joy!

A woman ordered a plate of oysters in a seafood restaurant. She told the waiter, "I'd like them not too large, not too small; not too salty, not too fat; and they must be icy cold." After a brief pause, she added, "And I want them quickly."

"Yes, ma'am," replied the waiter, "and would you like them with or without pearls?"

It's so easy to focus on our own needs and wants and ignore those of others—especially in a society where materialism and instant gratification seem to be the norm rather than the exception. "What's in it for me?" "If it feels good, do it." "I don't want to get involved." These common phrases of our time reveal the same sickness of the soul: narcissism, or self-centeredness.

But Jesus lived and taught another way. He said, "Whoever wants to be first must be last of all and servant of all" (Mark 9:35).

Look through the eyes of Christ today. Who needs your love and care?

Help me, Lord, to become a servant of all.

A baseball fan, with popcorn in hand, was returning to his seat. He stopped and asked the woman at the end of the aisle, "Did I step on your feet when I went out?"

The woman smiled, ready to accept his apology, and said, "As a matter of fact, you did."

"Good," he said as he squeezed past her. "Then this is the right row."

A little boy became quite angry with his friend and declared that he would never forgive her. When his mother encouraged him to make up, he said, "No! She never said she was sorry."

Every parent's hope is that his or her children will learn to have a forgiving spirit, like the father in the story of the prodigal son. He rushed to meet his son long before the son arrived. Hardly hearing his son's stammered phrases, he gathered him into his arms, restoring him to his place in the family. This is the way God welcomes us; can we do less for those we feel have wronged us?

Lord, help me to have a forgiving spirit.

POLICE

McPHERSON

What am I supposed to do with this?" an irate man asked as the police clerk handed him a receipt for his traffic fine.

"Keep it," the clerk advised. "When you get four of them, you get a bicycle."

"What's this?" we ask when confronted with the consequences of our actions. Have you ever tried to track down the source of an odor in your kitchen? So often it turns out to be something hidden away from view. No amount of "surface" cleaning will remove the odor; you must first find and remove the problem.

Instead of trying to ignore the consequences of our actions, we must face them and clear them out. A good place to start is on our knees, asking God not only to remove the stains our misdeeds have caused but also to help us make our daily actions more love-centered.

God, help me base my actions on love for you.

A man eating in a fine restaurant complained to the waiter that the lobster on his plate was missing one claw.

"I'm sorry, sir," said the waiter, "but our lobsters are so fresh, they fight each other in the kitchen."

"Well, take this one back," he said, "and bring me one of the winners!"

We've heard it said again and again: "It's not whether you win or lose, but how you play the game." How many of us really believe that? How many of us actually *live* it?

As Christians, we are to strive to be winners in the kingdom of God rather than winners in the eyes of the world. We are to be more concerned about our eternal reward than we are about the temporary rewards and riches we accumulate on earth. The apostle Paul wrote, "Forgetting what lies behind and straining forward to what lies ahead, I press on toward the goal for the prize of the heavenly call of God in Christ Jesus" (Philippians 3:13-14). There is no greater prize!

Keep my sights on your kingdom, Lord, so that my life may be pleasing to you.

MCPHERSON

A man returned to the drugstore where he had purchased some mothballs the day before. The clerk remembered him and asked, "Did you get rid of the moths?"

"No!" cried the angry customer. "I sat up all night throwing the balls at the moths, and I didn't hit a one!"

We may not throw mothballs at moths, but we act just as ridiculous when we stubbornly try to solve our problems our own way—without God's help. We don't seek God's advice through prayer, and yet we're angry when our "solutions" don't yield results.

When we refuse to carry our burdens to God in prayer, we often find that those burdens become even heavier to bear. Paul's words to the Philippians are a good reminder: "Do not worry about anything, but in everything by prayer and supplication with thanksgiving let your requests be made known to God. And the peace of God, which surpasses all understanding, will guard your hearts and your minds in Christ Jesus" (4:6-7). God will hear our prayers and meet our needs.

Loving God, help me relinquish control of my life and always bring my concerns to you in prayer.

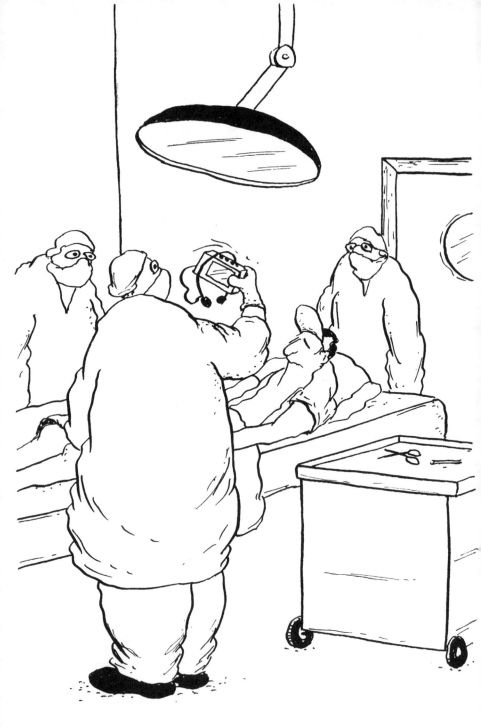

The doctor cured my hearing problem," one teen said to another.

"What did he do?" the other one asked.

"He removed my Walkman!"

Do you have on spiritual earphones? A good way to find out is to ask yourself how long it has been since a friend confided in you. Have you become aloof and unapproachable? How long has it been since *you* confided in a friend? Have you closed yourself off from others and from God, declaring by your actions that you believe yourself to be self-sufficient?

Think about some nagging problem in your life. Ask for God's help. Ask for a friend's help. Then open your ears and your heart and receive.

Lord, open my heart and my ears to your voice.

A young man walked into a jewelry store and told the clerk he was looking for an engagement ring. The clerk took out a tray of rings and stood back to allow the man to make his choice. The young man picked up a ring and asked the clerk, "How much?"

"That ring is $1,500, sir," he said.

The young man was astounded and gave a piercing whistle.

When the young man picked up another ring and asked the same question, the clerk replied gently, "That ring, sir, is worth two whistles."

Some things are so valuable that they are beyond our limited financial resources. But God's love, the most priceless treasure of all, is available to everyone! We don't have to earn it; in fact, we couldn't if we tried. God's unlimited, unconditional love is a gift, freely given to each of us. All we have to do is accept it. That's the good news that Christ came to share with us. It's such good news that we should want to share it with others!

Thank you, God, for your priceless love.

MCPHERSON

A golfer came into the clubhouse, panting, to meet his friend. The friend asked, "Why are you so late?"

"Because I had to toss a coin to decide whether to play golf or mow the lawn," he replied.

"I still don't understand," the friend said. "Why are you so late?"

"Because I had to toss it 17 times!"

We often pray, "Not my will but thine be done," but we seldom really mean it. We go to God in prayer with a specific answer in mind, and if we do not receive that answer, we keep praying, waiting for the answer we want.

E. Stanley Jones in *How to Pray* (Nashville: Abingdon Press, 1943, p. 20) reminds us to thank God for answering in his own way: "God will answer that prayer. No prayers are unanswered. But he may answer 'no,' as well as 'yes.' 'No' is an answer, and it may really be next in order leading on to 'yes.'"

If you have been waiting for a specific answer, stop and listen for God's voice. Perhaps God has already answered, and you have refused to listen.

May I listen and accept your answer, Lord.

A woman dropped her contact lens in a full wastebasket. She looked for it diligently, but could not find it. Her husband took the basket and soon found the lens.

"How did you do that?" she asked.

"Well, you were looking for a small piece of plastic. I was looking for $125!"

Jesus told a parable about a woman who lost a coin and threw a party after finding it. After finding her lost money, why would she spend it on a party? Some have suggested that the coin might have been part of a headdress of coins, given to the woman on her marriage. In that case, the coin was certainly more precious to her than its intrinsic value.

Likewise, each of us is precious in the sight of God. If we withdraw from the love of God, God will miss us just as badly as the woman missed her coin, and will search for us just as diligently.

Lord, thank you for welcoming me back when I have withdrawn from your love.

Little Donny saw his grandma's fingers, twisted with arthritis, and said, "Don't worry, Grandma, I'll get a hammer and straighten them out for you."

Grandma probably wishes that life was so simple! Life is frequently twisted and painful. As children, we want so much to grow into adulthood. But the minute we get there, we discover that adulthood comes with its own set of problems. In fact, no stage of life is free of them—not even childhood. Yet we seem to be able to navigate the storms of life more easily as children.

When we encounter life's challenges, may we keep the elasticity, simplicity, and hope of children.

Dear God, give me the spirit of a child—carefree, trusting, and hopeful.

A family from the Northeast went on vacation to Colorado. One night they ordered pizza from their hotel room. Five-year-old Andrew kept asking his father when the pizza was going to get there. Finally he asked his father nervously, "Daddy, do you think they know we're in Colorado?"

Sometimes we may feel that God is far away and that we have been forgotten. If you are having those feelings, ask yourself, "Does God go on vacation? Has God moved?" You may feel a little silly, but it will cause you to think.

Of course God doesn't take vacations. Of course God hasn't moved away. Why, then, are you feeling that distance from God? Could it be that you have "moved away" by neglecting your prayer life? Could it be that you have taken a "vacation" from helping others? In what ways are you the presence of God for someone else? And who might see the face of God in you?

Thank you, God, for always being with me.

A four-year-old girl was gazing intently at her great-grandmother one day. At last she asked, "Granny, are you a lot older than my mother?"

"Yes, dear," her great-grandmother replied, "I'm a lot older."

Nodding her head, the girl said, "I thought so. Her skin sure fits her better than yours does."

That great-grandmother probably chuckled and admired her great-granddaughter's powers of observation and innocence. And what a powerful combination that is. Children have the amazing ability to see and understand simple yet powerful truths—truths that, for us, often lie buried beneath years of difficult and disappointing relationships and experiences. As insulting as her remark may have sounded, no doubt this little girl, secure and comfortable in her great-grandmother's love, grasped this basic truth: It's what's inside that counts—not the packaging.

O God, thank you for using children to remind us of simple yet amazingly profound truths.

Amy told her family that she had learned in school that we are all made of atoms. Her little brother, Andy, protested, "No, we're not! I'm made of Adams; you're made of Eves."

What do you think of when you read the words "in the image of God"? What do you imagine God looks like? Most of us would shy away from saying that God looks like us. We might imagine a gentle teacher, perhaps like our favorite Sunday school teacher, a loving parent, or a king, sitting on a throne surrounded by angels.

But if God's work is to be done here on earth, then God must look like me. God's hands must be my hands. God's feet must be my feet. God became flesh in Jesus Christ. Since God was manifested in Jesus, then he is manifested in me as well. I must live my life so that when others look at me, they see God. I must use my feet, my hands, my heart, and my resources to bring about God's kingdom here on earth.

God, I was made in your image. Use me to do your will.

McPHERSON

At a family reunion, much was made of one-year-old Maddie. She had so little hair that her mother had taped a bow on her head to show that she was a girl. Maddie's grandfather said that she had about as much hair as he did.

Maddie's brother spoke up, "But Grandpa, her hair is coming, and yours is going!"

Ah, perspective is everything! Every task you hate is favored by someone else. Every person you dislike is someone's loved one. What is trouble to you is challenge to someone else. That is the way life is organized. We just have to accept the fact that there are some things we must hate.

Or do we? Perhaps we can change our perspective. How can we find the good parts of a disagreeable task? How can we look at the unpleasant acquaintance and see someone's best friend? How can we profit from the trouble? If we can't change the world, we may need to change our perspective!

Change my perspective, Lord, and help me find the good in all things.

A shipwrecked sailor who had been alone on a tiny island for months was elated when he saw a ship approaching. He watched with excitement as a rowboat was lowered from the ship and began to make its way to shore. When the rowboat arrived, two officers from the ship tossed the sailor a bundle of newspapers.

"Captain's compliments," one of them said. "You're to read these and then decide if you really want to be rescued."

What thoughts enter your mind as you read the daily paper or watch the evening news? Sometimes it seems that things are going from bad to worse. Yet hasn't this world always been a difficult place to live in—filled with greed, violence, tragedy, and misfortune?

God doesn't promise to prevent us from experiencing the bad things of this world, but God *does* promise to help us endure life's hardships and find true joy and peace. Through the gift of his Son, God has rescued us from sin, despair, grief, and hopelessness. We are never lost or alone with Jesus Christ as Lord and Savior of our lives!

Lord Jesus, fill me with your hope.

The bus was crowded, but one more man was pushing the others, trying to get on board. One angry passenger shouted at him, "Hey! The bus is full! Who do you think you are?"

The man replied, "I'm the driver."

"Come into my heart, Lord Jesus," some of us prayed or sang as children, "there is room in my heart for you." Is there room in your heart now for Jesus? Or, like the people on the bus, are you missing an important person on your daily travels?

Resolve this week to invite Jesus to go with you. Spend five minutes each morning thinking about the day as a gift that comes from God. During the day give yourself the satisfaction of doing one thing you have never given yourself time for. Enjoy a walk, write a letter to an old friend, or call a new acquaintance. Before you go to bed, add this line to your nighttime prayer: "Thank you, Jesus, for the blessings of this day."

Lord Jesus, may I always leave time in my schedule for you.

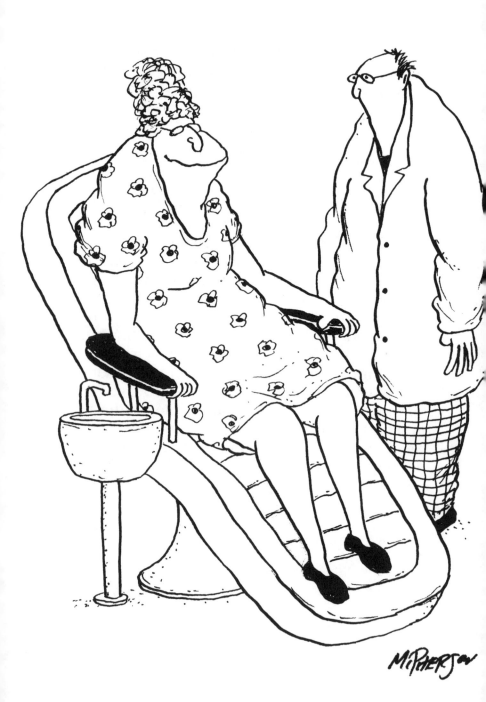

A young dentist had had an awful morning with mostly young patients who wouldn't keep their mouths open. His last patient of the day was a woman, and he greeted her effusively with, "Welcome! I can't tell you how pleasant it is to work on someone with a big mouth!"

We've all done it. We speak before thinking and then realize that what we've said isn't what we intended to say at all! We know from experience that words are powerful, having the force to hurt or to heal; yet so often we choose our words carelessly. Proverbs warns us: "When words are many, transgression is not lacking, but the prudent are restrained in speech" (10:19).

Beginning today, cultivate the habit of restrained speech. Take time to think before you speak, and choose your words carefully. Ask yourself if your words would be pleasing to God and how your words would make you feel if you were on the receiving end.

May all my words be pleasing to you, Lord.

McPHERSON

A grandmother decided to send a new playpen to her granddaughter for the birth of the granddaughter's fourth child. A week later the grandmother received a thank-you note.

"Thank you for your thoughtfulness," the granddaughter wrote. "I sit in the playpen for an hour every afternoon, and the children can't get near me!"

A widowed mother ate dinner with her six children every night, but she never joined them for breakfast. Once the food was on the table and the morning prayer had been said, she left the room. Because she had always done it, the children thought nothing about it until visits in other homes brought it to their attention. When questioned, the mother explained that it was the only time of the day she could be assured of a few minutes to spend alone with God. "I need that time," she said, "to thank God for the days that have passed and to ask for strength for the days ahead. Without it, I feel I am struggling alone."

If you feel you have been struggling alone, find a few minutes that you can be assured will be uninterrupted time with God.

Lord, thank you for always being there to refresh and strengthen me.

I'm warning you," said a piano teacher to an unruly student. "If you don't behave, I'll tell your parents you have talent!"

Are you sharing your talents and gifts with others, or do you hide them away? Perhaps you think you have been given no special talent or gift, but careful thought will reveal that you have something to offer. Could yours be the gift of a cheerful spirit? Use it to lighten the moods of others. Perhaps you have the gift of organization. There are any number of volunteer organizations—not to mention the church!—that would be very grateful for the sharing of that particular gift.

Gifts and talents come in a wide variety. We all have them; we all should share them.

Dear Lord, help me to recognize and use my special gifts.

McPHERSON

As a woman was walking across a parking lot, she saw a driverless car rolling toward her. With unusual agility, she opened the door, got in, and pulled up the emergency brake. As she got out, a man with his shirt sleeves rolled up was among the fast-gathering crowd.

"Well, I stopped the car!" she announced with pride to the man.

"I know," the man replied. "I was pushing it!"

So often we act impulsively, giving little or no thought to the reasons for our actions or their possible outcomes. Most of the time it is our impulsive responses to the routine events of our daily lives that get us into trouble.

Do you allow negative emotions to determine your reactions to people and situations? Try giving yourself a little distance from your emotions, stopping to think and pray before taking action. When faced with a decision, do you usually "go with your first thought"? Next time say a short prayer, asking God to help you decide what to do. When we pray, we open every moment of our lives to the wisdom and power of God.

Dear God, help me make prayer a vital part of every day.

A politician told a reporter, "I think the number one problem in this country is that no one wants to accept responsibility for anything. But don't quote me on that!"

Responsibility, reliability, trustworthiness, accountability—all are marks of a disciple of Christ. When we truly trust in God and God's promises, we are not afraid to say or do what is right.

The tenth chapter of Hebrews reminds us that we are to encourage one another and persevere in confidence, enduring whatever public persecution we might experience as a result of doing God's will. Beginning with verse 36 we read, "For you need endurance, so that when you have done the will of God, you may receive what was promised. For yet 'in a very little while, the one who is coming will come and will not delay; but my righteous one will live by faith. My soul takes no pleasure in anyone who shrinks back'" (vv. 36-38). As faithful followers of Christ, we must be willing to take a stand, even when everyone else "shrinks back."

Give me confidence and endurance, Lord, so that I may follow you faithfully each day.

A couple was driving in an extremely desolate part of the country and stopped for gas. The woman asked the attendant, "What do you do around here for excitement?"

He answered politely, "Ma'am, around here we don't get excited."

That same statement might be said by many Christians! There's nothing more contradictory than an unenthusiastic Christian. The Bible tells us that God loves us—so much, in fact, that he gave his only Son so that all who believe in him might have everlasting life. Nothing—not even death—can separate us from God's love! If we really believe that, we can't help overflowing with joy.

A faithful Christian missionary said that you are not responsible for the face you were born with, but you are responsible for the face you die with. When Christ lives in our hearts, our faces radiate his love to everyone around us. What do other people see when they look at your face?

Lord, help me be an enthusiastic Christian, sharing your love and joy with everyone I meet.

McPherson

A man bought a mousetrap for his basement. When he went down to set it, he realized he had forgotten to buy any cheese. So he cut a picture of cheese from a magazine and placed it on the trap. Surprisingly enough, it worked. When he went down to check the trap the next day, he found a picture of a mouse!

Being a Christian is hard. Helping a stranger when you might be putting yourself in danger; telling the truth when no one else is willing to take a stand; giving your time and talents to the church when you already have too much to do—these things are not easy. But you can't fool God. Looking the other way when you pass someone in need; saying nothing at all rather than speaking with honesty and integrity; and feigning new responsibilities in order to excuse your lack of involvement in the church will not fool God. God doesn't want a photograph of a Christian; God wants the real thing.

Dear God, help me to be an authentic Christian.

Two neighbors were visiting one evening. One of the women asked, "After a long, busy week, do you ever wake up grumpy on Saturday morning?"

"No," replied the other woman. "That's the day I always let him sleep in."

Jesus had a difficult life: born in a stable, poor all his life, misunderstood by his own family, betrayed by his own followers, hung on a cross. This is not the picture of a joyful life, yet Jesus had much to be joyful about: loving and tender parents, worshipful followers, dear friends, and a loving heavenly Father.

Jesus laughed often and had a good sense of humor. He once said that it would be easier for a camel to pass through the eye of a needle than for the rich to get into heaven. And he was no stranger to parties. In fact, he was criticized for hanging around with the "partying crowd." Was life hard? Sure. But Jesus lived it joyfully. So can we.

Giver of joy, help me to live each day joyfully.

The doorbell rang and Joe answered it, finding his old friend Ted standing next to a very shaggy and muddy dog. Joe invited his friend in, and they went into the living room to talk about old times. The dog jumped onto the expensive couch and then curled up for a nap—much to Joe's displeasure.

Finally, Ted rose to leave. As he went out the door, Joe asked, "Aren't you forgetting your dog?"

"He's not my dog," replied Ted. "I thought he was yours."

How often we jump to our own conclusions. Rather than getting to know a new coworker, we judge her according to the lastest office gossip. Rather than offering to help a stranger in need, we assume that he has already called for assistance or that someone else will surely lend a hand.

Wrong assumptions can cause us to hurt others—as well as ourselves. Often it is our wrong assumptions that prevent us from following Jesus' command to love our neighbors as ourselves.

Dear God, forgive me for making wrong assumptions and fill me with your wisdom.

Amid the many elaborate floats in a city parade was a simple flatbed trailer pulled by a farm tractor. On the trailer were several men wearing overalls, busily sawing and hammering boards together. The bystanders were puzzled until the float passed and they saw a sign on the back that read: "We thought the parade was next week."

Many of us are guilty of procrastination. We put things off until the last minute. Unfortunately, many of us are also "procrastinating Christians." With every good intention, we promise that next week or next month or next year we will commit ourselves to regular prayer, Bible study, worship, and Christian service.

Yet Jesus calls us to follow him *today.* When one would-be follower of Jesus asked if he could first bury his father, Jesus replied, "Follow me, and let the dead bury their own dead" (Matthew 8:22). We must be prepared to follow Christ today and every day.

I want to follow you, Lord Jesus. Show me the way.

A grandmother was taking her grandson to the movies. She suggested that he put a treat of some kind in her purse to munch on during the show. About halfway through the movie, the little boy leaned over to her and said, "Grandma, may I have my ice-cream sandwich now?"

Life has many surprises! Not all are pleasant. Sometimes by careful communication we can avoid surprises, but not always. How we deal with the surprises in life is crucial.

How do you think Grandma reacted? She could have caused a major scene by yelling. Or she could have shut out her grandson with angry silence. A much better reaction, however—perhaps after a moment of shock— would be to accept some of the responsibility and break into laughter. Always looking for the "smile" in a difficult situation helps defuse an explosion and build a solution.

God, help me handle the unsettling surprises of life with laughter.

Kevin's father smiled when Kevin knocked on the bedroom door early one morning and said, "Today's Nerd Day at school, Pop. Can I borrow some of your clothes?"

Kevin's father could hardly be pleased by this expression of his son's opinion about his clothes! Yet he isn't seriously worried about his son's feelings, either. He knows of his son's love and respect when Kevin asks for help on his homework or when he so attentively listens to his dad's advice on how to properly swing a baseball bat.

Kevin and his dad have a firm foundation for their relationship, and it has nothing to do with Dad's nerdy style of dressing. So it is with our relationship with God. It may not always look great, but underneath it all is the intimacy and protection we all seek from a loving parent.

O God, thank you for keeping me safe and secure in your loving care.

Badly bruised and scratched, an employee staggered into his workplace one hour late.

"What happened to you?" yelled his irate boss.

"I fell down a flight of stairs," he said.

"And that took you a whole hour?" his boss asked.

In one of his best-known parables, the parable of the good Samaritan, Jesus showed us what it means to have mercy on another human being—regardless of race, class, or "public opinion." He ends the parable by saying, "Go and do likewise" (Luke 10:37).

How compassionate are you? Try this experiment. For the next seven days, begin and end each day with these verses from 1 Peter: "Live in harmony with one another; be sympathetic . . . compassionate and humble. Do not repay evil with evil or insult with insult, but with blessing" (3:8-9 NIV). Then say a short prayer, asking God to increase your compassion. God will not disappoint you!

O God, give me a compassionate heart.